Why should I?
EAT POWER PROTEINS

Cindy Devine Dalton

The Rourke Book Co, Inc.
Vero Beach, Florida 32964

PHOTO CREDITS
Village Beach Market, Vero Beach, Fl.
Gibbons Photography

EDITORIAL SERVICES
Pamela Schroeder

Library of Congress Cataloging-in-Publication Data

Dalton, Cindy Devine, 1964-
    Eat power proteins / Cindy Devine Dalton.
       p. cm. — (Why should I...)
    Includes index.
    Summary: Describes the different kinds of proteins and how they affect our bodies.
    ISBN 1-55916-304-6
    1. Proteins in human nutrition—Juvenile literature. [1. Proteins. 2. Nutrition.] I. Title.
II. Series

QP551 .D25 2000
613.2'82—dc21

00–028019

Printed in the USA

CONTENTS

We need to eat protein every day.
Protein makes our bones sturdy and our
muscles strong.

WHAT IS PROTEIN?

Have you ever thought about your muscles and bones? How do they grow? What makes babies strong enough to stand and walk? What helps you pick up a heavy rock or swing a big bat?

Protein is a **compound** in food that makes our muscles and bones grow healthy and strong.

ANIMAL PROTEINS

Protein is in two kinds of food. One source of protein is from animals. Animal proteins are in foods like meat, cheese, milk, and eggs. Can you think of foods you eat that come from animals?

Cheeseburgers have a lot of protein in them. The hamburger and the cheese are both animal proteins.

PLANT PROTEINS

Another kind of protein comes from plants. Plant proteins are in foods that grow out of the ground. Beans, vegetables, and rice all grow out of the ground. Plant proteins are **incomplete** proteins. They are good for us, but they do not give us all the protein we need.

Beans, vegetables, and rice are incomplete proteins.

VEGETARIANS

People who do not eat meat are called **vegetarians**. Vegetarians must make sure they get enough protein. They can get all the protein their bodies need if they combine vegetables, beans, and rice. If vegetarians only eat vegetables, they will not get enough protein.

Vegetarians are people who eat only vegetables. There are many good vegetables to choose from! A great snack for vegetarians is celery and peanut butter.

Meat is power packed with protein.

Cheese and dairy products are a good source of calcium and protein.

13

PROTEIN AS ENERGY

Protein helps our bones and muscles work well. It keeps us strong and **sturdy**. Protein also gives us energy. Protein helps us play and exercise without getting too tired. Can you think of something good to eat before you play? Pick a food that has a lot of protein in it. If you guessed peanut butter or nuts, you're right!

Beans are a great source for protein. They give us a lot of energy for play and exercise. They also have a lot less fat than red meat.

HOW MUCH TO EAT

Eat two to three **servings** of proteins every day. Remember, complete proteins are eggs, fish, meat, cheese, and milk. If you eat one egg, two slices of bacon, and a glass of milk for breakfast, you are meeting your **requirement**.

Do you think this is a lot of protein? You bet it is! There is enough protein in a steak to meet your daily requirement and more.

THE FUN IN HEALTHY

When kids are having fun, they are using protein. Protein gives us energy. Kids who play hard and exercise need as much protein as adults. Kids who are tired and irritable may not get enough **nutrients**. Nutrients are proteins, fats, carbohydrates, and vitamins. Kids need a lot of nutrients to have fun and stay healthy.

Could you play without energy? Protein gives us energy to play hard and have fun.

HAVING FUN IN THE KITCHEN

Learning to eat healthy can be fun. You can share your food ideas with your parents. Parents enjoy their children helping in the kitchen. How can you help your parents plan a **menu** that is healthy and fun? Try to pick a different food for every meal for five days. Wow, that means you will probably eat a lot of new foods!

Parents like having help from kids. You can tell your mom
or dad what you like and help plan the menu.

To play and feel good, you need protein.
Kids play better together when their bodies
are well fed with nutritious food.

22

GLOSSARY

compound (KAHM pownd) — parts added together to make a whole

incomplete (IN kum PLEET) — missing a part

menu (MEN yoo) — a list of dishes served at a meal

nutrients (NOO tree entz) — foods that cause growth and repair

requirement (rih KWYR ment) — something that is needed

serving (SER ving) — a helping of food or drink

sturdy (STER dee) — firmly made or built

vegetarians (VEJ eh TAYR ee enz) — people who eat a diet that is made of only vegetables. Sometimes fish and chicken are also eaten

FURTHER READING

Microsoft Encarta 98 Encyclopedia
The New Complete Medical and Health Encyclopedia,
    Volume Three 1996 856-879
Healthwise Handbook, Kemper, Donald W. 1995 253–268

INDEX